Duckweed
浮萍

Duckweed
浮萍

poems

Kathryn Lennon
姚君妍

Library and Archives Canada Cataloguing in Publication

Title: Duckweed : poems / Kathryn Lennon = 浮萍 / 姚君妍.
Other titles: Duckweed (Compilation) | 浮萍
Names: Lennon, Kathryn (Poet), author.
Series: Crow said poetry.
Description: Series statement: Crow said poetry ; 15 | Includes some text in Chinese.
Identifiers: Canadiana (print) 20260162299 | Canadiana (ebook) 20260162329 | ISBN 9781774391495
(softcover) | ISBN 9781774391501 (EPUB)
Subjects: LCGFT: Poetry.
Classification: LCC PS8623.E585 D83 2026 | DDC C811/.6—dc23

NeWest Press wishes to acknowledge that the land on which we operate is Treaty 6 territory and Métis Nation of Alberta Region 4, a traditional meeting ground and home for many Indigenous Peoples, including Cree, Saulteaux, Niitsitapi (Blackfoot), Métis, Dene, and Nakota Sioux, since time immemorial.

Editor for the Press: Wendy McGrath
Book design: Céline Chuang
Author photo: Jordon Hon 韓寶軒

NeWest Press acknowledges the support of the Canada Council for the Arts, the Government of Alberta through the Ministry of Arts, Culture and Status of Women and the Edmonton Arts Council for support of our publishing program. We acknowledge the financial support of the Government of Canada through the Canada Book Fund for our publishing activities.

NeWest Press
10131 97 Street
Edmonton, Alberta T5J 0L2
www.newestpress.com

Printed and bound in Canada
1 2 3 4 25 26 27 28

For 姚羅煥好*,*
姚慧玲 *Wai-Ling,*
and 姚君純 *Gwun-Shun.*

"So I roam backward and forward across the continent. When I am East, my heart is West. When I am West, my heart is East. Before long I hope to be in China. As my life began in my father's country it may end in my mother's.

After all I have no nationality and am not anxious to claim any. Individuality is more than nationality. "You are you and I am I," says Confucius. I give my right hand to the Occidentals and my left to the Orientals, hoping that between them they will not utterly destroy the insignificant 'connecting link.' And that's all."

—Sui Sin Far (Edith Maude Eaton),
"Leaves from the Mental Portfolio of a Eurasian."

Dear reader, some notes about language

廣東話 gwong^{2} dung^{1} waa^{2} Cantonese is my grandmother and mother's mother tongue. My grandmother and mother were, and are, also literate in traditional Chinese characters. When I hear Cantonese, or see Chinese characters, I feel both a sense of comfort and familiarity, but also a sense of being an outsider. I am nowhere near fluent or literate. My experience with Cantonese is through the filter of it being spoken, and lived, in lands that were/are British colonies, thus I have often experienced it alongside English, as well as alongside Mandarin. I learned some Mandarin as a child, because it was accessible in Edmonton's public school system.

Throughout this collection, I have attempted to use Cantonese and traditional Chinese characters in ways that are true to my own experiences of them. This means that sometimes my use is inconsistent, messy. Sometimes it may take effort for you to decipher, sometimes you may feel connected.

My inspiration for how to represent traditional Chinese characters within these pages includes: signage in Hong Kong, and in Edmonton's and Vancouver's Chinatowns, labels on food packaging, and children's workbooks. My inspiration for how to represent Cantonese phonetically comes from how I've heard the language spoken around me: in restaurants; at family gatherings; overhearing my mother on the phone; in my grandmother's house in Hong Kong; and in the streets and shops of Chinatowns.

In some poems, I use informal transliterations that echo how I've seen the language reflected around me. In others, I use Jyutping (the Linguistic Society of Hong Kong Cantonese Romanization Scheme), mainly in places where I don't trust my own transliteration will make sense to you. In some places I've painstakingly used online dictionaries including Yellow Bridge, Pleco, and Jyut Dictionary, and relied on help from my mother, and friends, to confirm both formal and colloquial word choices and meanings. Mistakes are all my own.

I have chosen to include a glossary of some words. There are a few other languages used throughout, that are not my family languages—Japanese, Mandarin, and Cree—for those I have tried to name sources for my knowledge of them.

Contents

1.

A Crack in a Tongue

Duckweed 浮萍: Variations on a Proverb

人生像浮萍

"People often use this proverb to describe life with little or no root, so they are wanderers, or life is so unpredictable that they are like duckweed 浮萍 that go with the flow of water in ponds and have little control of where they would be going."

—Wai-Ling Lennon, my mother

一

A floating
lotus, unaware
I am anchored by roots.

I don't know where
to begin, unsure
what's forgotten.

人
生
像
浮
萍

"Life is like duckweed" - Google translate

二

Illiterate in my mother's proverbs:
this one is about duckweed,
not a lotus, she points out.

三

I am
common

duckweed
expansive on

still water,
ubiquitous.

I am not
a lotus blossom.

I should have known
better.

Daughter Tongue Twister

Unspoken things between us.

This lack
becomes a gap

a black hole of language,
a complicated
kind of rage trapped
in the brains' backrooms,
hearts' closets.

This daughter's tongue ties
tries to find the words,
but they stick
in her teeth
like bits of meat: she lacks
a toothpick.

She tries
to speak the words,
but they slip from her lips
like
grains
of
rice: she lacks
a placemat.

This daughter's tongue gets stuck.
Unsure how to unfold
that language of the gut
with this language of the brain.

This daughter's tongue gets stuck
on sing-song tones, homonyms, homophones,
synonyms, proverbs, and ancient poems—
a language of puns and wordplay she'll never get.

This daughter wonders if it takes a lifetime of living
wrapped in context, syntax and rhythm,
teahouses, markets and temples
to truly know it in larynx, tongue and hyoid bone.

This daughter's tongue does not speak
her mother's mother tongue,
or her father's mother's mother's mother tongue.
She has tried. Is trying. Will keep
trying. Why? Why try to speak
a language not required in her day-to-day life?

Because she wants to know:
what the old books teach
the poets speak
the revolutionaries preach.

Because she wants to know:
names of rivers
mountains
cities she may never see

what the grandfathers laugh about under the trees
what the grandmothers gossip about over their tea.

She looks in:
rice-cooker kitchens
railroad ties and shipping yards
side-streets of nation
alleyways of empire
grandparents' wardrobes
sewing machines
and silence.
She looks in the throats of
the colonies
the colonized
the colonizers
skyscraping skylines
countrysides
islands
and coastlines.

She looks in all the places
we grew up speaking differently.
In the hearts of us who seek
languages we think we should speak
as if those languages will fix
a crack in a tongue
a gap in a lung
a shortage of spirit
a crooked tooth
split lip
as if

those languages will tune
our tongues, and sync
us to some universal beat.

But after all this,
she comes to see
that language is not
talisman, trinket, or party trick.
Not some chip you can stick
in your brain and just press play.
There is no quick way:
it has to be learned.

She sees that language won't
fix anything until
bloodlines and borders
become irrelevant
until we stop saying what
we are not
we cannot
and start saying what
we are
we can
we will.

She comes to see
nothing is inherent.
Language takes courage
because, like anything else,
it has to be learned.

She comes to see
that learning to speak
is like learning to eat.
Rolling vowels like melon seeds
from the backs of our mouths.
Tuning taste buds to different frequencies
and sending words over our teeth

flying out into the world.

To Mend a Gap

長洲 *Cheung Chau,*香港 *Hong Kong, 2011*

There is a sewing machine
passed down from my
太 婆 to my
Taai^{3} Po^{4}
媽 媽
Maa^{1} Maa^{1}
that has waited on my

婆 婆's balcony
Po^{4} Po^{4}

over mountains and across an ocean
for twenty years for
my clumsy too-big hands to
thread the bobbin and hesitantly
slide
fabric
under sewing machine foot
twist the knob tap the pedal
with my too-big foot
coax hesitation into hum

s - t - i - t - c - h together frayed edges
to mend a gap.

長洲 *Cheung Chau,*香港 *Hong Kong, 2008*

My mother picks up the telephone
her words travel across time zones
from a sweaty receiver, through
undersea cables to land on

my father's ears.
She asks him to find a newspaper
clipping, the only copy of the only
interview about

公 公
Gung^{1} Gung^{1}'s life

My father will find it at the bottom
of a bedside drawer under
paperclips and phone bills, mail it
express across the Pacific Ocean

so it will arrive in time
for the cremation,
so the words pressed
into newsprint can travel
into the afterlife

婆 婆
Later, Po^4 Po^4 will call him
鬼 佬
and though his gwai^2 lou^2
ears will not receive
all of her words

唔 該 晒
her m^4 goi^1 saai^3 will mend a gap.

I Wish I Could Be Careless

could care less
not carry the muscle
memory of migration
at the base of my neck

but I fear a future of
forever facing forward
forehead forgetting the passing of time
is told by breaths of mitochondria
and birth of cells.

It seems implausible to believe my tears will find the sea
until I remember these floorboards
once too had leaves.

Someday I Will

擔心 daam sum		set down this worrying
小心 siu sum		this smallness
點心 dim sum		learn I am more than the sum of these parts
中心 zung sum	心	lubdub this heart in some centre I can't get to
用心 yong sum		with care and carefulness
開心 hoi sum		open these walls
放心 fong sum		be free

Yong Sum 用心 Use Heart

To be diligent, attentive, careful; with motive, intention.

My mother tells me this in our yellow kitchen,
scratching

用心

blue pen on white paper.

Too much forgetting who we are,
forgetting to use both head and heart,
together, instead taught to keep
them segregated,
lest we love too much.

2.

Dragons Might Have Been Here

二

apihkês

"Where I am from in Alberta, a Chinese person is called 'sêkipatwâw', which means 's/he has braids'. This gives you a fairly good idea of when this name began to be applied to describe the appearance of early male Chinese migrants. Another name is apihkês, which actually means 'spider'. I have been told this refers to weaving skill."

—Chelsea Vowel[1]

She's learning to time travel
to wind the threads
back on spools from which they've unwound.

She's learning to untie
tongues
land
railroad tracks
pipelines.

---

1 Reproduced with permission of HighWater Press (Winnipeg), from *Indigenous Writes: A Guide to First Nations, Métis & Inuit Issues in Canada* by Chelsea Vowel (© 2016 Chelsea Vowel and HighWater Press).

She's learning to untie
can-nots
do-nots
are-nots
should-nots.

She's learning to spin storylines and lifelines and laughlines
to tie together frayed ends of old threads
to weave webs that hold up the sky.

Dragons Might Have Been Here

Dragons might have been here once
but we would never know
'cause the footprints that they might have left
are covered by the snow.

This is a poem for the
train tracks.

This is a poem for the broken backs.
This is a poem for the broken bones
that line the Fraser River bed.

Under every foot of track in the Fraser Valley
lies the body of one Chinese railroad worker.

This is a poem for the train tracks
built on the backs of mountains.
For the train tracks built to build a nation.
The train tracks built to build a dream.

This is a poem for the
train tracks.

For the tracks that splintered spines of rocks
tracks that splintered spines of Chinamen.
For the train tracks built
on the backs of coolies.

This is a poem for the
broken bones.

For the train tracks built
on the broken backs.
Bones snapped
like chopsticks.

This is a poem for the bones
that never made it home.

This is a poem for the
heads taxed.
For the yellow bodies less than white.
For those with less than equal rights.

This is a poem for the
lines laid on the backs of coolies.

For stories that line faces of grandparents
who won't speak to save face.
Who faced seas, mountains, wars.
Whose faces will never appear on the face of our $5 bills.

This is a poem for the
ties that bind
that break our feet, backs, spines, spirits.

We are like railroad ties, laid out in parallel lines,
invisible lines that stop us from seeing
that collectively we are the track
that bears the load of each passing train.

We are the track
that underlies this economy

where the undesirable work
has long been done by the undesirables
where the skeletons under our cities are shades
darker than the faces in the board rooms.

These race lines, these power lines, these rail lines
are the cracks in the foundations of this nation's heritage.

In the "Canadian Heritage Minute: the Last Spike!"
They're all white.
Out of sight, out of mind in the back were the Chinamen,
silent spikes who broke their backs for these rail lines.

Selective amnesia
creates collective amnesia

makes us internalize invisible lies learned by heart,
by skin, by bone,
that tell us we are not at home,
we don't have a stake.

These train tracks would not exist
were it not for the backs of Chinamen.

This is a poem for the silent spikes.
Whose stories weren't shared.
Whose shame, pride, strength, and hope
the future might be different kept them silent.

Dragons might have been here once
I'll tell you how we know
'cause the footprints that they
left are where the wildflowers grow.

Maan Maan Sik 慢慢食

Cast of Characters

There is a lot that remains unknown about these characters.

太公 TAI GONG:

Born in China. He comes to Canada as a labourer. His wife and young children are in southern China, he is unable to reunite with them after the passing of the Chinese Immigration Act (Chinese Exclusion Act) of 1923.

婆婆 POH POH:

Born in southern China in 1921, she never meets TAI GONG (her father). But she immigrates to Canada with her husband in 1950, after the Exclusion Act has been repealed. They run a café in a small town.

阿媽 A-MA:

Born in Canada in 1955, POH POH's daughter. A teacher.

孫女 SYUN LUI:

Born in Canada in 1988, A-MA's daughter. A poet.

ACT I

July 1, 1923: Humiliation Day. Scene opens with TAI GONG *sitting alone on a folding chair at a mahjong table, eating bitterness* 吃苦 *hek³fu².*

TAI GONG:

Exclusion begets a shutting begets a shattering
begets isolation begets fraternity.

Exclusion begets grief begets resignation
begets forgetting begets determination.

Exclusion begets determination begets ambition
begets integration begets assimilation.

Exclusion begets debt begets resilience
begets ingenuity begets wealth.

Exclusion begets resistance begets remembrance begets
competition begets exclusion.

ACT II: Scene 1

2023. One hundred years since the Chinese Exclusion Act was passed. A-MA is standing alone in her kitchen, rice cooker and wok in front of her, preparing dinner. Backdrop is coloured by catastrophe, genocide, and a kind of racism that's shifted shape but still perpetuates their foreignness. Against this, their lives keep unfolding.

A-MA:

There are no days off to sit with this weight and ponder
who we are as Chinese Canadians,

who we might have been were our momentum not interrupted
by a quarter-century of splintered families. Forced bachelorhood.

Who we might have been, were we not handed humiliation
by the Department of Immigration and Colonization.

Now, even though we can swim and vote and work,
we can't unpeel the labels:

perpetual foreigner yellow peril model minority.

ACT II: Scene 2

Today. SYUN-LUI *sits alone on the living room couch, writing poetry in a notebook.*

SYUN LUI:

Now, I understand your silence.
I think I see now how it might take
a generation, or two
or three, or four,
before the silence cracks open
like a century egg.

Cracked open, it reveals an opaque centre,
an ambiguous inheritance
we are left to pick at in the
high definition light of our present day.

ACT III

Near future. SYUN-LUI, A-MA, and POH POH sit at the kitchen table together with TAI GONG's ghost.

POH POH: Maan6 maan6 sik6 慢慢食.

SYUN LUI: What does that mean, mom?

A-MA: Eat slowly, like bon appétit.

SYUN LUI (laughs): Eat slowly so you don't choke on the bones.

A-MA (laughs): Exactly.

SYUN LUI: It's hard to imagine what one hundred years from now will look like, and how we might get there.

A-MA: I hope we'll have gone deeper than inclusion, that your children's children's children will be seen simply as human.

TAI GONG: That they won't measure their worth by their work.

SYUN LUI: That they will no longer need to turn their collective community energies and creative minds to the work of repealing and resisting and reacting.

TAI GONG: That they will gather around the table and, rather than eating bitterness, they will maan maan sik.

They linger after the bowls are clean of rice and soup, alternating between wiping the tears rolling down their faces, and laughing as they hold their bellies.

Come West

Come west, young man
and seek your fortunes.
Opportunity awaits.

Come west,
to a wild land of freedom. Famed
for its vast plains, claim a piece for you.

Come west, to a land where
big trucks, big malls, big stuff
like giant Ukrainian Pysanky
and UFO landing pads
welcome you.

Come to a land named after a British Princess,
though these places already had names.

Wetaskiwin: place of peace
Athabasca: place where there are reeds
Okotoks: crossing to the big rock.

Come west to a land
where petroleum vampires suck
the spark from our eyes
where crude awakenings
make dinosaurs roll in their graves

where ghosts of resources extracted,
exploited, extirpated,
linger.

Come west, young man,
believe an industry that invites, entices
with money like you would not believe.
Believe Suncor, Shell, and Syncrude
who spin crude tales out of truths
about tailings ponds that leave toxic trails
in our bodies, water, land.
Believe a government who spins crude tales
to make believe cancer rates downstream are irrelevant.

Come west, young man,
to the city I grew up in but don't recognize anymore,
because cranes are straining for a sky getting higher
and higher, because it's ringed by refineries,
like teen beauty queen tiaras that wink and glitter
spilling sprawl into the night.
This is the prize you seek.

Here young man, you will watch
as a mosquito siphons blood from the buttocks
of the last bison that shits on the lost
shin bone of some undiscovered dinosaur,
drowned in bitumen.
Young man, you will roll down the window
of your god-given pick-up truck,
aim the barrel of your gun,
and pull the trigger.

But we will say:
no.

Overhead powerlines
will become the charged
sweetgrass sage peace pipe
lines of palms
lines of power.

Thunder will gallop in,
chasing butterflies over the prairie edge
between the backwards blink
of birch branches.

We will say:
no.

Dene, Cree, Métis treaty lands
leased to tar sands industry.
Train tracks laid
by Chinese.
Black pioneers
forced off their farms.
Buffalo meat left to rot
by European settlers.

We say:
no.

The pressure of 4.5 billion years of
crushing, faulting, stratification
is released. This land re-covered with bison,
boreal forest, parkland, grassland, foothills, muskeg.
Rivers unwind.
Rocky Mountains unfold.
Canadian Shield melts to magma,
and cast-off carapaces expand
until the sea floor again crawls with crustaceans.

So, young man,
if you chase the sun west
east of the mountains
above dreaming dinosaurs and buffalo bones
where the wind in the leaves of aspen trees is the sea,
the skies will open

you will breathe again.

Come west and
dance hip hop
hip to hip
among the wild rosehips
down by the river.
Come west and line dance
down yellow highway lines.
Maybe you will find your fortunes
if you drive out past the city lights.
Maybe you will turn off the highway
to stands of pines and arrive at a lake
where the sunset splits the sky

under banks of clouds
and you will lay with your cheek to the ground
open your eyes to the orange slice of horizon
as stars freckle the dark, high above
ducks scatter up off the water
the north star rises
the moon comes up
all you will know is that you are here
on this soil
under this sky.
You are small
and this is too big.

You cannot own this.

Three-inch Golden Lotus 三寸金蓮

The crack of toe bones breaking
for the sake of beauty, the crack
of toe bones breaking
to create feet like lotuses
like feet were never meant to be
this never happened to me.
Our grandmother's feet were never bound.
They never broke her bones
never told her that her feet were lotuses.
Our grandmother's feet were tough.
They carried her as she walked
through war to sell wares,
bring money home to her family.
When she married, her city feet
became island feet, bare feet
carrying water from well to field
on her husband's farm. Her feet
became vegetable selling, child carrying feet.
Her feet were never broken, they were never bound
but she was bound to a time when a woman
did not choose whom to love, she was bound
to a society where women were worth
less. She did not break these rules.

Our mother's feet were never bound.
They never broke her bones.
Never told her that her feet
were lotuses.
Her feet were vegetable selling,
basketball playing,
sandy beach feet,
sneaking-out-to-go-dancing-at-night feet.
Bound to carry her away feet,
from a society where women do not break the rules.
Her feet carried her onto a plane,
across an ocean,
across mountains,
becoming university student feet,
winter boot feet.
Her feet were never broken, they were never bound,
but she was bound
to break the rules. It became a balancing
feat learning to stand strong
straddling the world she'd left behind,
and the life she'd chosen here.
Her feet became standing-at-the-front-of-a-classroom-feet,
learning-to-ice-skate-feet, buying Chinatown groceries feet.
They knew no bounds.
But she was bound to a time
when not all women had the same choices,
now bound to a place where she was less than white.

My feet were never bound.
My bones never broken.
I was never told my feet were lotuses.
My giant feet.

When I was a kid
I wished I could have broken
the toes off my too-big feet.
I couldn't stand the feet
that made me
stand out
stand up,
stand taller
than everyone else.

My feet kick
point
run
climb, never bend
into lotuses.

But I am still bound
by double binds
that tell us we're not shaped the right way
make us accept less than equal pay
make me bound to say
to you, sister:

Never let those bindings bend
our spirits, never let them break our power.

Our feet were never broken, never bound,
happiest when toes are free, these feet
are strong, stand out, stand up, stand tall feet.
They are choose-your-own-adventure feet,
and they will never let us fall.

Tong Yun Gaai 唐人街

102 AVENUE

The river edge lands replaced

by laundries and restaurants replaced

by Canada Place replaced

by Harbin Gate replaced

by a pagoda-roofed train tunnel

myopic downtown revitalization

and lazy public consultation
to replace

geopolitical sisterhood to replace

blight-clearing urban renewal to replace

brotherhood of railroad labourers required
by colonial operations

to replace kinship and buffalo networks.

Memories are slippery in this
shifting space that has been
rebranded a thousand times.

But you still remember the multicultural centre 點問頓中華文化中心
gymnasium where you bowed to the audience along
with your classmates, children of Vietnam, Brunei, Laos, Singapore,
Burma, Malaysia, Hong Kong, Taiwan, China, and performed
Gong-Xi-Gong-Xi in your fluffy red vest and double pigtails.

You remember the smell of fresh-ground ink, your cramped hand
gripping bamboo brush, your wobbly strokes, and the tea breaks
with your calligraphy teacher.

You remember the theatre
where your aunties watched Sunday movies, tossing
peanut shells to the floor.

You remember the second-floor restaurant with pearl in its name,
where your parents held their wedding reception and forgot to pay
the bill.

You remember the togetherness of Double Greeting 七喜小食店
wonton mein lunches with your poh poh, walking her back to the
Elders' Mansion, past proud signage of ancestral villages and the
ancestors' names

			台	開
馬	黃	朱	山	平
Mah	Wong	Gee	Toi Shan	Hoi Ping

and her favourite statue of 孫中山 Dr. Sun Yat-Sen.

97TH STREET (NAMAYO AVENUE)

In the neighbourhood of mythical beasts
and free parking,

紅色
the colour of tenacious fortune
cop car lights and lanterns
firetrucks and lamp posts and blood
and gates of happy arrival.

藍色
the colour of translucent strength
wide winter skies
tarped homes and needle casings
and rubber-band-clamped lobster claws
in aquariums in restaurants
with chipped porcelain teacups.

黃色
the colour of displaced dignity
old world pride and new world shame
objectification and vacant lot
dandelions and DAAN TAAT
and GAI MEI BAO and the phone books
we sat atop of for bowlcuts.

綠色
a colour harder to find
flecks of cilantro in steaming beef balls
basil atop steaming PHO
the abandoned artists' garden
atop the abandoned railroad bridge
faded flat grass in the park
named after the Black Angel of Boyle Street.

Through fire, plague, death, and pests,
we always return for DIM SUM
at the restaurant reborn
a thousand times, across the street
from the park with the faded flat grass.

I'm no longer sure how to be
in this place that has helped fill
our home with the things we call home,
lined our shelves with the scallop brine
smells of distant oceans,
heaped our tables with steaming SIK FAAN
portions of our mother tongues,
provided the YUM TONG soup bone
foundations for every meal.

Our elders worked so hard
to grind meat, print newspapers, press DOU FU,
they never look up to see
if we are following behind them.

While colonial figureheads play God of Wealth
and anointed patriarchs squabble annually over
LAI SEE in the banquet halls,
another life or livelihood or lifeline is lost.

But on cracked concrete
you, my friends,
you are saving a life
walking with a grandmother
sharing steamed buns
painting a mural
planting seeds.

3.

Hundred Tastes on Your Tongue to Solve Your Homesickness

三

Recipes for Young Cooks

魚

jyu[2]

Ginger, sliced,
green onions criss-crossed
over steamed white fish in black bean
sauce with rice and Kraft

Dinner bacon iceberg lettuce tomatoes
Kraft Golden Italian Dressing toast.
I never realized how involved Kraft
was in my upbringing.

花

faa[1]

Cooking is confusing when
the stomach wants something
but the head doesn't hold words
to describe what these ingredients will become
I don't know
what will happen when the
pressure of cooking to bridge

a gap will make us rely on cardboard food
which feeds us
though our taste
buds will not
flower.

薑

goeng[1]

Ginger is a root.
I don't know what to do
with(out) it. I don't know
what I can(not) say. Every

thing I cook is from scratch.
I am defeated by the mounds
of Ontario apples at the grocery store
and go home empty

handed because ginger is
imported from China.

心

sam[1]

We don't cook by heart
we think we make our
selves every day
following allrecipes.com
and *Company's Coming* cookbooks.
They sure fooled us.

Gai[1] Daan[2] Zai[2] 雞蛋仔 Chicken Egg Kid

This heart cracks open
like a chicken egg sunset
sunny side upside sundown
upset.

It's easier
to separate white
from yellow folks
than it is to separate egg whites
from yellow yolks.

Uprise
sunrise fry up rise up
like a chicken egg sunrise
scramble this heart.

Foreign Persimmons 西红柿

西红柿 *fānqié :*	*tomato, western red fruit or western persimmon (Mandarin)*
番茄 *faan[1] ke[2]:*	*tomato, foreign or barbarian eggplant (Cantonese)*

i.
Six storeys above parking lot,
nine above sidewalk,
(how many metres above flood plain?)
I am wasting precious water
on foreign persimmons.

I should give them more soil to stretch their legs,
protect their parched roots so they will stand tall,
so this water won't run off,
like second-hand love,
to the balcony below.

The ancestors can't fathom why
we half-barbarian offspring yearn to grow
something to remind us of how they laboured
skin dark in sun
bare feet on earth.
My bare feet step on
smooth finished floor
carrying tap water from sink
to pour into potting soil
hoping gravity will guide it to
root.

ii.
Too much yeet hay 熱氣.

I shouldn't have passed up the Whole Foods
pay-by-weight salad bar for a Wendy's
Jr. Bacon Cheeseburger, fries and Frosty,
childishly nostalgic for the nights when eating out
meant driving to a fast food joint
planted in parking lot.

There are different ways to please the soul.

iii.
The red fruit sun
pleads to be plucked
from burning sky
set down
on concubine earth
to sip cool water and roll in shade
but the earth burns too
longs to be lifted up
to catch a breeze
slip through stratosphere,
spin in space.

Hunger is Inherited

I see my mother's mother,
squatting on a newspaper in our kitchen
her hands folding
bamboo leaf triangles around sticky rice.

I see my father's mother,
sitting by a window in a red dress
her hands unpeeling
Kraft singles.

I've gone searching for recipes
in kitchens of other grandmothers
only to find them stuck
like tea leaves to the sides
of my cup.

Until the only thing left to do
is to visit the only grandmother left.
I cross the world
to see Poh Poh.

Now, here, I sit, hoping she'll speak to me.
Hoping she'll teach me
hoping she'll spill kitchen secrets
of black beans, cornstarch, and soy sauce
brought to a boil,
thickened.

But what I learn instead:
to thicken my skin
so her words will not hurt me.

My grandmother's skin
is paper-thin, blue veins raised like
remnants of the great wall
and I wonder if her great wall
of stubbornness will ever fall.

She falls more often now,
has broken both hips, hit her head.
The arches feet once planted
in the street, selling vegetables,
bok choy, gai lan, choy sum,
no longer steady her.
But she is stubborn and fear of falling
is nothing compared to fear of failing
to feed one's family.
She still remembers hunger.

She worries I'm hungry,
gets up to shuffle into the kitchen
and I follow, hoping
I will find kumquats preserved in salt
after the New Year, hoping
I will find secret maps tattooed

onto the backs of my hands,
maps that will let me
crisscross checkpoints and bypass borders
trading secrets for spices and spices for seeds.
But, the kitchen is small.
I'm too tall.
I don't know
how to hold a knife,
how much rice to cook for two,
I don't know
the names of vegetables.

She tells me, get out of the way!
From the sidelines, I watch her
rinse rice,
slice wintermelon,
heat peanut oil in wok,
crisscross green onions, ginger, soy sauce
across fish belly.

My belly has never known
hunger. Yet, I am afraid
when the last Saskatchewan farmer
yields to Monsanto
we won't know how to feed the cities.
When the grandparents are gone,
our tongues will long
for food we no longer know
how to name.
The food we eat will feed us
but our taste buds will not flower.

I am afraid to tell her why I'm here.
Afraid to say: Poh Poh, I'm hungry.
Hungry for recipes for survival
to help me hold out against the
day-to-day doubts that come from
not knowing the words to name my hunger.
Hunger for the wisdom of women who
carry the weight of the world on their hips.
Hunger, because if I have a daughter,
I don't know what colour
her skin will be or what language
she'll dream in, but
I'll need to teach her to
trust her gut,
find the food that makes her heart
and stomach fly.

But, I can't say this in Cantonese.
Luckily, I love to eat.

Now, it's six o'clock.
Fish is steamed, the neighbours are home, and the news is on.
So, I pour the tea, fill our bowls
as she shuffles out from the kitchen and takes her seat.
I turn to her and say the only thing I know how to say,

婆婆食飯
"Poh Poh, sik faan"

eat rice, grandmother.
And we eat.

Ritual

1.
Let your feet take you to Chinatown
唐人街
to the bakery recommended to your mother
by the owner of a Chinese bookshop.

Stare at the many flavours of mooncakes

月餅
as customers jostle you in slices
of Mandarin and Cantonese.

2.
They don't take debit,
you have no cash. Wander
surrounding blocks until you find an ATM.

Withdraw money. With gratitude.

3.
Return. The server will ask if
"lai sik gong, gwong dong wa?"
You respond,
"siu siu, gong siu siu."

She calls you, "lang lui,"
says you are, "ho lek."
She is impressed that you
"cho dan che."

4.
Buy two individually-packaged mooncakes.
You can't eat a whole box alone.
When asked if it's a gift, say,

"no, no, just for me,
no need to wrap it."

5.
Let your feet take you to the Sunny Spot Cafe,
greasy spoon with all-day breakfasts,
Xi'an burgers and biangbiang noodles.
The awning announces: 舌上百味解鄉愁
"hundred tastes on your tongue to
solve your homesickness."

Eat lunch.

Wish the owners a,
"zhōng qiū jié kuài lè."

6.
Let your feet take you to the corner grocer
with organic peanut butter, tortillas and
pomelos dressed in red ribbons. Buy one.

7.
Return, to your rented room.
Ask the internet to teach you
your traditions.

Follow a Facebook link. It tells you to
gather, give thanks for the harvest, share mooncakes.
One slice for each family member.
Wonder how you will eat a full one alone.

8.
Wikipedia tells you to make offerings
to Great Uncle Earth and Chang'e.
You have no incense.

As the story goes,
Chang'e swallowed the elixir of immortality
soared to the moon to become a goddess.

You remember your mother's
voice reciting these stories.
Chang'e placing the elixir of
immortality on her tongue and
fleeing through the
palace corridors.

9.

Let your feet take you to the kitchen.
Take longan, three candles, one mooncake.
Think of 李白 Li Bai's
"静夜思 Quiet Night Thoughts."

Let your feet take you outside,
kneel under the magnolia tree.
Lift your head and gaze at the bright moon 月.
Lower your head and think of home, wherever that is.

Lift your head and wonder how to pray.
Think of heaven 天.
Think of earth 地.

Break the mooncake in half,
salted yolk surrounded
by lotus paste.

Place it on your tongue.
Tell yourself you should enjoy it.

Recipes for New Mothers

WARM THE WOMB RED DATE TEA

For sipping in the lonely
middle of the night after pumping
breast milk like a bionic goat:

Take one handful each of

紅棗
red dates:
for warmth and strength
of blood and body.

龍眼
longan:
for peace, power,
and protection.

枸杞
goji berries:
for clear sight
and the life ahead.

Simmer in a pot of water
until the toughness softens.
Allow the steam to open up
conversation.

Tastes best when delivered in a thermos by your mother.

SMASH THE PATRIARCHY CUCUMBER SALAD

The quickest way to smash
cucumbers is with a cleaver.
Thwack. Thwack. Thwack!
Bits fly, land quick on the floor,
kitchen counter, your hair.

Mix with

芝麻油
sesame oil,

醋
vinegar,

豉油
soy sauce.

Equal
parts spicy, sour, salty.

SOMETHING FROM NOTHING
HAND-PULLED NOODLES 拉麵

Flour, water, salt.
Knead until all the feelings
are relaxed.

Rest.
Let time and gravity do the work.

Hotdog Fingers

—after Michelle Yeoh

From her overnight bag, my mother pulls
a pack of all-beef wieners.
For breakfast,
she halves them then slices them
lengthwise into quarters
fries them up so they shine in their own grease.

We eat them with scrambled eggs
and leftover congee.
Only a mother would have
so many hotdogs on hand.

I am reminded of the alternate universe
in *Everything Everywhere All at Once.*

Maybe the only way to achieve freedom
from domestic duties
is to exchange your fingers for the hotdogs
your family would have eaten.

4.

Saltwater City
鹹水埠
Haam Sui Fow

四

Saltwater City 鹹水埠 Haam Sui Fow

Here, tears in teacups
taste like rain. Slip out of skin
and swim to sunset.

Mornings, Under Mist

these mountains stay mum
lips pressed tight,
guardians of secrets

until I catch them
smiling against sunrise
twin sisters speak,
guardians of peace

then across inlet, I see
a pair of stone lions yawn
one mouth open
one mouth closed
mother and father
guardians of entrances

and I know why
this place feels old like home.

Wayfinding

1. NORTH END, OFF-RAMP, ARTHUR LAING BRIDGE

Silence speaks for itself.

This city
where there is a city before a city
where bones and waterways sing
under concrete and cobblestones and grass
where the steel slap clap of pigeon wings echoes off glass
where loneliness oxidizes iron in rain
where difference begets exclusion
begets ignorance begets disgust
begets displacement begets confusion begets rust.

2. EAST GEORGIA STREET, 200 BLOCK

Young, upright, hipsters carrying paper coffee cups stride
by old, bent-backed,
seniors carrying plastic grocery bags, shuffling
by construction crews who pound the ground.

Like barnacles,
the grandmothers and grandfathers
cling to habitat,
some more immune to erosion
than others.

They haggle loud
enough that I can hear them through the walls.

3. PAUERU GAI POWELL STREET, 400 BLOCK

There are many ways to erase
community.

Remove baseball players
from home base.
Replace.
Remove baseball diamond
from park.
Replace.
Displace its grandmothers.

Remove benches
from park,
bricks from walls.
Replace.
Misplace names.
Forget their names.
Rename.
Assimilate.
Replace.

Name it something historic.

4. LADNER EXCHANGE

It's in the little words.

The:

ands, but, befores.

The:

all, is, ors.

These streets are glowing cherry pink,
but it's only February.

Before there were urban planners there were planners.

This city will be for you and you
and you and you and you and you.

It's not about belonging
or not, it's what you do with it, with your place in it all.

A Moment of Silence for Phuong Na Du

—for Phuong Na (Tony) Du 余臘芳

when you fell
on wet road

did you see boats
on slow-moving rivers

your mother picking through bean sprouts
grinding rice into milk

did your teeth bite sky
like lychee flesh

did you feel sweet beans
slide down your throat

did your fingers reach
for the hands of uncles

did you hear bullets
break your skin

yellow burst
like sunrise over rice fields?

Chinatown South HA-1A Redevelopment

You can't hold a neighbourhood
in the palm of your hand
like a snowglobe.

You can't shake it to see generations yet to come.

You can't freeze it
in a state of red
cheeked celebration
hands clasped in eternal
New Year's greetings
performing stiff-legged routines
to an emptying room.

It would be kinder to let it unravel.

Let its grandchildren
bear witness
as memories shutter their doors and
nostalgia papers over its windows.

Let them come forward
oranges in hand
to light incense
at the altars of rezoning applications.

They will re-develop
postures of defiance.
They will grow their hair long.

They will swim upstream,
through grief, and love, and rage,
shedding skins, swallowing water,
in search of the source.

Tomb Sweeping Day 清明節

Lok yu 落雨.
It is raining.

I don't know where the bones lie,
but the salt water I swallow and
the bright white crocuses

remind me it is time
to sweep the ancestors' tombs
and give my love

to the living.

5.

Both 來 *and Going*

五

Persistent Process

My feet will me to estuary 河口海口.

To both 來 and going. Both
開 and narrowing. Both
end of 河 and start of sea.

A grandfather stops to look north at 山
then pluck juice boxes
sprouting from garbage can
like fireweed
flaming from roadside.

A jogger stops to look west at 水
then stretches one leg
like blue heron brush stroke
balancing in place.

I am learning my parents are not encyclopedias,
my father will lose the names of trees
and my mother will lose the names of food,
that as they are forgetting
I am memorizing
to meet rising tide and pounding rain.

Mid-Autumn 中秋

White is a forgetful way of life,
as in: blank slate,
as in: erase your own histories,
assimilate your differences,
swallow your stories.

You can choose not to live this way.
I am grateful to those of you who choose not to live this way.

To the knowledge keepers and knowledge seekers,
the ones with the caverns in your chests:

thank you

for spitting out stories

for insolence

after five generations of eating
white food you still hold your heads up high
and ask
why should I swallow this?

for gentleness

for sifting through histories with shaking hands
until you can hold them without breaking
bones

for subversion

submerged you've learned
to float
to shapeshift
to slip out of skin
and swim upstream

for persistence

abandoned you've patiently
tended tidal pools
until meaning floods in

for grace

you've let knowledge stick to you
like burrs
carrying it
to safer ground
where come autumn the
grandchildren will
gather for the harvest

Islands in the Shape of Nations

There are islands in the shape of nations in our blood.

I feel my fingertips crinkling and toe pads wrinkling
waters rising,
coastlines eroding.

The moon
doesn't call the tides
like it used to.

The rain
doesn't fall
to the earth like it used to.

It feels like we are boats
with no moorings
sailors with no stars.

We need to go farther
from shore to find
fish these days.

Typhoons toss cars
crumple concrete
swallow cities
bend rooftops

like bamboo
these roots hold on.

In Transition

立春 START OF SPRING MONTH

You come out into the world nonchalantly
an unexpected home birth in the dark hours
of a frigid lunar new year's eve.

We grew you last summer on food from our garden:
peas, spinach, kale, chard, beans, corn, tomatoes, potatoes.
Cherries from the backyard, berries from u-picks.
Black chernozemic soils around our city.

We are learning all the names of things
our mothers call babies in their mother tongues:
baby shrimp, baby duck, baby bear, baby cat.

I wonder who you will be, who you will love, who will love you.
I wonder what your relationship will be to this land.
I wonder what world you will live in,
what seasons you will live with,
how you will move through it all as it all falls apart.
I hope we can fill you with enough love
to float your life raft through it all.

清明 CLEAR AND BRIGHT MOON MONTH

Stop reading the news. Turn off your phone. Get out of bed. Breathe in and out, and in and out. Pull on some jeans, boots, socks optional. At least this morning, while the light is honey and blue, set down your grief, leave it on the kitchen table in the dish where you keep spare change. Pull out those seeds your ancestors carried in their pockets as they fled war, famine. Open the door, set one foot in front of the other. Step out onto cracked concrete and the muck and grit and skeletons of last year's leaves. Greet the hare with one eye. Greet the irises pushing up so green it hurts. Pick a piece of earth, small enough to love. A terracotta pot, an old milk carton, a strip of land, a raised bed. Make a plan or follow your instincts. Pull your fingers through the soil. Scatter seeds. Add water. This is enough for today.

穀雨 GRAIN RAIN MONTH

I let you play with a Pyrex container. You drop it and it shatters
into smithereens. Dust. I'm not able to stop you, my son,
though I watch it in slow motion. What have we done?

秋分 AUTUMNAL EQUINOX

We take you to the forest, the ocean, the river.

The world sparkles into focus
as you discover the power of naming:

Puppy.
Garden.
Cheese.
Flower.
Birch.
Moon.
Stars.

Jo Sun, Poh Poh

Jo sun Poh Poh
Good morning, Poh Poh.
早晨婆婆。

Ho loi mo geen
Long time no see.
好耐無見。

Lai sik joa fan?
Have you eaten yet?
你食咗飯?

Goh doh yum cha
The dim sum over there,
嗰度飲茶,

Ho m ho a?
Is it any good?
好唔好呀?

Ngo you go zai
I have a son now.
我有個仔。

Keoi gam nin leong sui.
He is two years old.
佢今年兩歲。

Kui sik gong siu
He knows how to speak a
佢識講少少

Siu gwong dong waa
little Cantonese.
廣東話。

Jong yee yum cha,
He likes dim sum,
鍾意點心,

Sik faan, sik juk,
rice, congee,
食飯, 食粥,

Sik mein, dou fu
noodles, tofu,
食麵, 豆腐,

yong fai ji la.
to use chopsticks.
用筷子啦。

His name means ocean,
so he won't forget
where we come from.

I wish you could
have met him. But
I suppose you have,
when we bai sun,

bow to your photo
atop my parent's TV stand
offer you flowers and
navel oranges. I'm sorry

I haven't set up
an altar for you
in my own house.
I keep meaning to.

Sometimes I think of
you and burn incense—
did you get the
messages I left you?

Acknowledgements

My deepest gratitude to the places, people, and communities I have written about, who held me up while I moved as a guest through your ancestral lands, especially— 長洲 Cheung Chau, 香港 Hong Kong. wîhkwêntôwin neighbourhood and the Papaschase reserve lands I live in within amiskwacîwâskahikan, Edmonton, Treaty 6 Territory. Vancouver, Chinatown, and the Paueru Gai Areas, within the unceded territories of the Skwxwú7mesh (Squamish), Səl̓ílwətaɬ (Tsleil-Waututh), and xʷməθkwəy̓əm (Musqueam) Nations. Victoria, on the traditional territories of the Lək̓ʷəŋən (Songhees and Xʷsepsəm/ Esquimalt) and W̱SÁNEĆ peoples. Kitchener-Waterloo, in the Traditional Territory of the Chonnonton, Neutral / Attawandaron, Anishinaabeg, and Haudenosaunee Peoples, on the Haldiman Tract. Thank you for inspiring me with your placemaking, language and culture reclamation, and decolonizing work. Thank you to the beautiful Chinatown, Chinese and Asian arts communities of these places in all your diversity.

Thank you to my family for all the love and support: my mother for your bottomless knowledge and passion for sharing culture and language, for translating and proofreading the Cantonese. My father, for being the first to ever edit my writing. My sister, for receiving and appreciating some of these poems in their rawest forms. Abu Y, teslam edek, for helping me protect the time and space for poetry in this era of too little sleep, and to the Zs who have become the threads pulling these poems forward. Our Hong Kong family for opening your homes to us and looking after us on countless visits: Poh Poh, Gong Gong, Kau Fu, Kau Mo, Biu Ze, Biu Go, Yee Yee, Yee Zoeng, Yee Ma, my Biu Muis, and Biu Dais. Aneh, Guido and the Amtos and Ammos for all your love and support. Our West Coast family, for your support in my time in your city: Cousin S. & J., Aunty A. and Uncle B., Aunt M. and Cousin M. Thank you to the writers, editors, readers who shared knowledge and experience: Alexis K. (for your ongoing mentorship). Kimmy B., the Writers' Guild of Alberta (and Peter M.), Neil Aitken, and Rachel S. for providing edits and feedback on early versions of this manuscript. Yilin W., for working so thoughtfully with my mother on the co-translation of many of these poems – even though we haven't been able to use them yet, our countless conversations about Chinese language and poetry really impacted me. Christine W. for sharing your experiences of working with Cantonese in published poetry. Kyla P. for checking my use of Cree. To the writers ahead of me who shared knowledge that helped light the path of the poetry publishing process, Marco M., Iman M., and Adriana O.

Thank you to the world-building poets who created the spaces that gave some of these poems their roots and wings and first audiences: the *Breath in Poetry Collective* (Titi, Mary, Ahmed), my fellow *2012 Edmonton Slam Team* members (especially Medgine and Sara), the *Victoria Festival of Spoken Word*'s Missie and Dave (and my fellow poets), and the *Canadian Festival of Spoken Word.*

Thank you to the friends, community builders, collaborators, and creatives who were part of the Chinatown communities and moments some of these poems grew out of: Paul G., Sharon Y., Freya F., Mike L., Yvonne C., Kristin C., Doris C. and June C. and the Youth Collaborative for Chinatown, Sweden X., Zoe L., Sarah L., Jane S., Szu S., Carven L., Christina L., Candie T., Lydia K., Rita W., Claudia L., Kevin H., Nicole S., Megan L., Chanel L., Christopher C., Peggy L., Natalie T., Tyler R., Victor N., Anna LK., Kathy S., Daniel I., Dennis G., Meika T., Justin W. And Keren T., Emily C., Shawn T., Daniel H., Jordon H., William L., Will CM.,

Yihua Z., Lee L., Jinzhe C., Stephen T., Wei W., Lan CM., Jyn-Ting Y., and Jia Jia Y.

Thank you to friends who encouraged me, broadly. To the ones who were there around kitchen tables with me before these poems were anything to hold: Asha P., Rachel S., Emily C., Linda S., Ashlea HV., Alyssa R., Jenny C., Taarini C., Renée M., Reena R., Bella L., Janice L., Vero DG., Rosabeth K., and Jayna M. To the ones who nudged and watched: Chris CYP., Trevor CF., Aly K., Julia D., Beth H., Malambo M., Azkaa R., Omar Y., Robin N., Nancy L., Jessica M., Mandy M., Marie S., Angelica Y., and Sandra N. To the aunties who divided the stresses and multiplied the joys and always fed me: Philiana W. and Catherine W (and thank you both for checking the Canto)., Karena D., Rose Y., Angeline Q., Jessica T., Jessica T., Emily C., Helen C., Grace K., Joanna K., Joanne P., Kerry T., Linda R., Sharon L., and Kathy T.

This book was supported by grants from the Edmonton Arts Council and the Edmonton Artists Trust Fund Award. By time and space at the Banff Centre for Arts and Creativity (and the Myra Paperny Endowment for Emerging Alberta Writers, with support from the instructors Sharanpal Ruprai and Suzanne Zelazo, and my cohort of fellow poets.

Thank you to the mighty team at NeWest Press: Meredith Thompson, Matt Bowes, Fawnda Mithrush, Christine Hassay-Kohler, and especially to Wendy McGrath, my editor, for her belief in these poems and championing and shepherding this manuscript. Thank you to Céline Chuang for the cover and book design, for transforming these poems into a physical thing of beauty.

Thank you to the editors, publishers, curators, and community builders who have given homes to earlier versions of these poems:

Hunger is Inherited." *Beyond Touch Sites: an Anthology of the Tangible.* Edited by Wendy McGrath. Laberinto Press, 2025.

"Foreign Persimmons 西红柿." Canthius. Co-translations by Wai-Ling Lennon 姚慧玲 and Yilin Wang 王艺霖. Fall 2023.

Yong Sum Use Heart." Polyglot, Issue 11: 用心. Co-translations by Wai-Ling Lennon 姚慧玲 and Yilin Wang 王艺霖. 2023.

"Three-Inch Golden Lotus" and "Dragons Might Have Been Here." Living Hyphen Magazine, Issue 2, Volume 1: Resistance Across Generations. Co-translations by Wai-Ling Lennon 姚慧玲 and Yilin Wang 王艺霖. 2021. *www.livinghyphen.ca*.

"Someday I Will." AlliterAsian: Twenty Years of Ricepaper Magazine (an Anthology). 2015.

"Food (In)Security" and "Feet Unbound." Ricepaper Magazine, Issue 16.1, "Generations." 2011.

"Wayfinding." The Ethnic Aisle, the Canada Issue. 2015.

"In Transition." *Reimagining Fire: the Future of Energy.* Edited by Eveline Kolijn. Durvile & UpRoute. 2023.

"Maan Maan Sik 慢慢食" originated from a poem commissioned for the Edmonton opening of the exhibition, "Eating Bitterness 吃苦: from Exclusion to Inclusion." 2024.

"Tong Yun Gaai 唐人街" was first published in "Untouchable Chinatown 脱俗不凡唐人街", a collective photography project and photo book, curated by Jordon Hon, 2023, and was inspired by the work and community care actions of my fellow artists in this project.

"Recipes for New Mothers" began as "Sitting the Month," a collaboration with Jia Jia Yong, performed at the Skirts A Fire Festival and Nextfest. 2022.

"Islands in the Shape of Nations" was used in the short film Islands in the Shapes of Nations (May mga isla na sa hugis ng mga bayan)", created in collaboration with Christopher J. Carter (visuals) and Tagalog translation (Dennis Gupa). 2014. *https://vimeo.com/102091191*.

Notes

1. Epigraph: Sui Sin Far, “Leaves from the Mental Portfolio of an Eurasian.” *Independent* 66 (21 January 1909): 125. *www.scribd.com/doc/258366471/Leaves-From-the-Mental-Portfolio-of-a-Eurasian*

2. p. 24 ("Dragons Might Have Been Here"): To learn more, read some of the stories, and see the faces of individuals and families directly impacted by the 1923 Chinese Exclusion Act, refer to *The Paper Trail: to the 1923 Chinese Exclusion Act* by Catherine Clement. Plumleaf Press. 2025.

3. p. 42 ("Tong Yun Gaai 唐人街"): I consulted the Chinatown Story Map for place names in Edmonton’s Chinatown. Chinatown Story Map. *www.chinatownstoriesmap.com*. Led, illustrated, and designed by artist Emily Chu. 2024.

4. p. 63 ("Ritual"): 李白 Li Bai was a Tang dynasty poet, and one of his most famous poems, and one that I learned as a child, is “静夜思 Quiet Night Thoughts.”

5. p. 69 ("Saltwater City 鹹水埠 Haam Sui Fow"): Haam Sui Fow 鹹水埠, or Saltwater City, was how early Toisanese settlers referred to Vancouver. Read more: Paul Yee. *Saltwater City: An Illustrated History of the Chinese in Vancouver.* Douglas & McIntyre, 1998.

6. p. 70 ("Mornings, Under Mist"): The “twin sisters” is a reference to the Skwxwú7mesh (Squamish) story of “The Two Sisters” as documented by E. Pauline Johnson-Tekahionwake in *The Legends of Vancouver.* Geo. S. Forsyth & Co. 1912.

7. p. 72 ("Wayfinding"): The area once known as Paueru Gai, the Powell Street neighbourhood in Vancouver's Downtown Eastside, was a place of early settlement and forced removal for Japanese Canadians, but also a site of regeneration. I learned it from friends involved with Vancouver's Japanese Canadian community and the Powell Street Festival, who have published: *Return to Paueru Gai: Fifty Years of Vancouver's Powell Street Festival.* Edited by Emiko Morita. Arsenal Pulp Press, 2026. Read more here: *powellstreetfestival.com*

8. p. 74 ("A Moment of Silence for Phuong Na Du"): Phuong Na (Tony) Du 余臘方 was a Chinese Vietnamese man who was killed by Vancouver Police Department officers on November 22, 2014. Read more about his story here: *https://savechinatownyvr.substack.com/p/remembering-phuong-na-tony-du*

9. Several of the poems in this collection were inspired by placemaking community work I was involved in as part of the Vancouver's Youth Collaborative for Chinatown, between 2014-2016. Earlier versions were first published as part of my Masters final project: Kathryn Gwun-Yeen Lennon 姚君妍, YOUNG HEARTS IN CHINATOWN 青心在唐人街: Activating Public Space in Vancouver's Chinatown, University of British Columbia, 2016. *https://open.library.ubc.ca/soa/cIRcle/collections/graduateresearch/310/items/1.0306868*

Glossary

I have included select words or phrases. You may have already figured out the meaning from context. Pronunciations are Cantonese, using the Jyutping romanization system, and everything is written in traditional Chinese characters.

太婆 taai^{3} po^{4}	maternal great grandmother
婆婆 po^{4} po^{4}	maternal grandmother, also poh poh or po po
媽媽 maa^{1} maa^{1}	mother
公公 gung^{1} gung^{1}	maternal grandfather
太公 taai^{3} gung^{1}	maternal great grandfather
阿媽 aa^{3} maa^{1}	mother
孫女 syun^{1} neoi^{2}	grand-daughter, also syun lui
鬼佬 gwai^{2} lou^{2}	slang for foreigners, white folks
唔該晒 m^{4} goi^{1} saai^{3}	thank you, for a service

唐人街 Tong^{4} Yan^{4} Gaai^{1}	Chinatown, literally Tang People Street
擔心 daam^{1} sam^{1}	worry
小心 siu^{2} sam^{1}	be careful
點心 dim sum	dim sum
中心 zung^{1} sam^{1}	centre
用心 jung^{6} sam^{1}	with intention, also yong sum
開心 hoi^{1} sam^{1}	happy
放心 fong^{3} sam^{1}	relieved, at ease
紅色 hung^{4} sik^{1}	red
藍色 laam^{4} sik^{1}	blue
黃色 wong^{4} sik^{1}	yellow
綠色 luk^{6} sik^{1}	green
魚 jyu^{2}	fish

花 faa1	flower
薑 goeng1	ginger
心 sam1	heart, also written as sum
熱氣 jit6 hei3	hot air, a state of being heaty in traditional Chinese medicine, also written as yeet hay
食飯 sik6 faan6	eat rice, bon appétit
慢慢食 maan6 maan6 sik6	eat slowly, enjoy your meal
河口海口	estuary, literally river mouth, ocean mouth
來	to come/arrive
開	to open
河	river
山	mountain
水	water

Kathryn Lennon 姚君妍 is a writer, editor, and community planner. Her poetry has been published in *Canthius, Polyglot Magazine, Living Hyphen, the Globe & Mail, Ricepaper Magazine,* and the *Ethnic Aisle,* among others. Her writing has been included in several anthologies including: *Reimagining Fire: the Future of Energy* (Durvile & UpRoute), *Back Where I Came From* (Book*hug Press), and *Beyond Touch Sites: an Anthology of the Tangible* (Laberinto Press). She is the co-founder and co-editor of Hungry Zine, a food-focused publication that centres voices missing in mainstream food media. She holds a MA from the University of British Colombia's School of Community and Regional Planning, and a Bachelor of Environment from the University of Waterloo. She has Cantonese and Irish heritage and lives in Edmonton, amiskwacîwâskahikan, within Treaty 6 Territory. *Duckweed* is her first full-length collection of poetry.